EXPLORING BIOMES
MARINE BIOMES

by Lela Nargi

Ideas for Parents and Teachers

Pogo Books let children practice reading informational text while introducing them to nonfiction features such as headings, labels, sidebars, maps, and diagrams, as well as a table of contents, glossary, and index.

Carefully leveled text with a strong photo match offers early fluent readers the support they need to succeed.

Before Reading

- "Walk" through the book and point out the various nonfiction features. Ask the student what purpose each feature serves.
- Look at the glossary together. Read and discuss the words.

Read the Book

- Have the child read the book independently.
- Invite him or her to list questions that arise from reading.

After Reading

- Discuss the child's questions. Talk about how he or she might find answers to those questions.
- Prompt the child to think more. Ask: Have you ever been to the coast or to an aquarium? If so, what kind of marine life did you see?

Pogo Books are published by Jump!
5357 Penn Avenue South
Minneapolis, MN 55419
www.jumplibrary.com

Copyright © 2023 Jump!
International copyright reserved in all countries. No part of this book may be reproduced in any form without written permission from the publisher.

Library of Congress Cataloging-in-Publication Data

Names: Nargi, Lela, author.
Title: Marine biomes / by Lela Nargi.
Description: Minneapolis, MN: Jump!, Inc., [2023]
Series: Exploring biomes | Includes index.
Audience: Ages 7-10
Identifiers: LCCN 2021060768 (print)
LCCN 2021060769 (ebook)
ISBN 9781636907628 (hardcover)
ISBN 9781636907635 (paperback)
ISBN 9781636907642 (ebook)
Subjects: LCSH: Marine ecology—Juvenile literature. Marine biodiversity—Juvenile literature.
Classification: LCC QH541.5.S3 N335 2023 (print)
LCC QH541.5.S3 (ebook)
DDC 577.7—dc23/eng/20211216
LC record available at https://lccn.loc.gov/2021060768
LC ebook record available at https://lccn.loc.gov/2021060769

Editor: Eliza Leahy
Designer: Emma Bersie

Photo Credits: Jag_cz/Shutterstock, cover (left); posteriori/Shutterstock, cover (right); Rich Carey/Shutterstock, 1, 23; Benny Marty/Shutterstock, 3; Alones/Shutterstock, 4; Eric Carr/Alamy, 5l; Daniel Zuckerkandel/Shutterstock, 5r; Jan Wlodarczyk/Alamy, 6-7; Allan Holland/Shutterstock, 8-9; Choksawatdikorn/Shutterstock, 10; Chase Dekker/Shutterstock, 11; Wirestock Creators/Shutterstock, 12-13t; Martin Pelanek/Shutterstock, 12-13b; Nature Picture Library/Alamy, 14-15; Anton_Ivanov/Shutterstock, 16-17t; Adam Ke/Shutterstock, 16-17b; Evgeniy pavlovski/Shutterstock, 18; Gerald Corsi/iStock, 19; Biosphoto/SuperStock, 20-21.

Printed in the United States of America at Corporate Graphics in North Mankato, Minnesota.

TABLE OF CONTENTS

CHAPTER 1
Salty Water...4

CHAPTER 2
Life in Layers..10

CHAPTER 3
The Ocean and Us.....................................18

ACTIVITIES & TOOLS
Try This!..22
Glossary..23
Index...24
To Learn More...24

CHAPTER 1
SALTY WATER

Which **biome** makes up 70 percent of Earth's **surface**? It is the marine biome. It is the biggest biome on the planet. It is made up of salt water.

Bay of Fundy

high tide

low tide

Most of this is ocean. The ocean has **tides**. Most coasts get two high and two low tides each day. Canada's **Bay** of Fundy has the highest tides. They are more than 50 feet (15 meters) high!

Red Sea

There are five ocean **basins**. These make up the Arctic, Atlantic, Indian, Pacific, and Southern oceans. Together, they make up one huge body of water! It touches all seven **continents**.

Seas are smaller parts of the ocean. They are partly surrounded by land. The Red Sea is between Africa and Asia. It connects to the Indian Ocean.

TAKE A LOOK!

Earth's five oceans are part of the marine biome. Take a look!

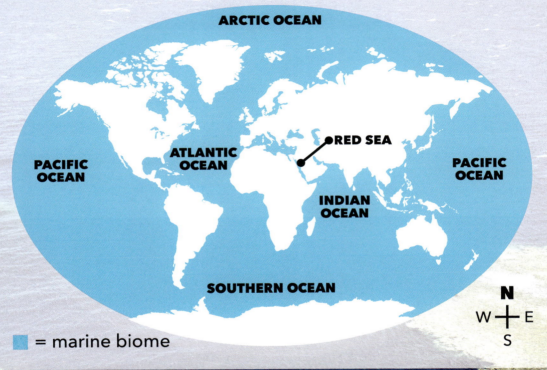

= marine biome

CHAPTER 1 | 7

Estuaries are where oceans meet rivers. The water is calm. It is full of food, such as oysters and crabs. Birds like herons raise chicks here. They have plenty to eat.

CHAPTER 2
LIFE IN LAYERS

Scientists have counted more than 228,000 **species** in the marine biome. They think there could be a lot more. **Plankton** live in this biome. They are tiny. Many ocean animals eat plankton.

plankton

Blue whales are Earth's biggest animals. Every year, they travel 4,000 miles (6,437 kilometers) to find food and give birth.

CHAPTER 2

sunlight zone

twilight zone

The ocean has layers. Each layer gets a different amount of sunlight. The sunlight zone is closest to the surface. It is **shallow**. It gets the most sunlight. Plants and **algae** grow here. Dolphins, jellyfish, and whales swim.

The twilight zone is next. Here, the ocean is deeper and darker. It is also colder. Why? It gets less sunlight. Swordfish and shrimp live here. Several kinds of octopuses and squid do, too.

Fewer species live in the midnight zone. Why? Sunlight can't reach these depths. Plants don't grow. There is less to eat. Giant squid, viperfish, and blobfish live here.

DID YOU KNOW?

Many marine species glow in the dark. This scares **predators**. It can also draw in tasty **prey**.

viperfish

CHAPTER 2

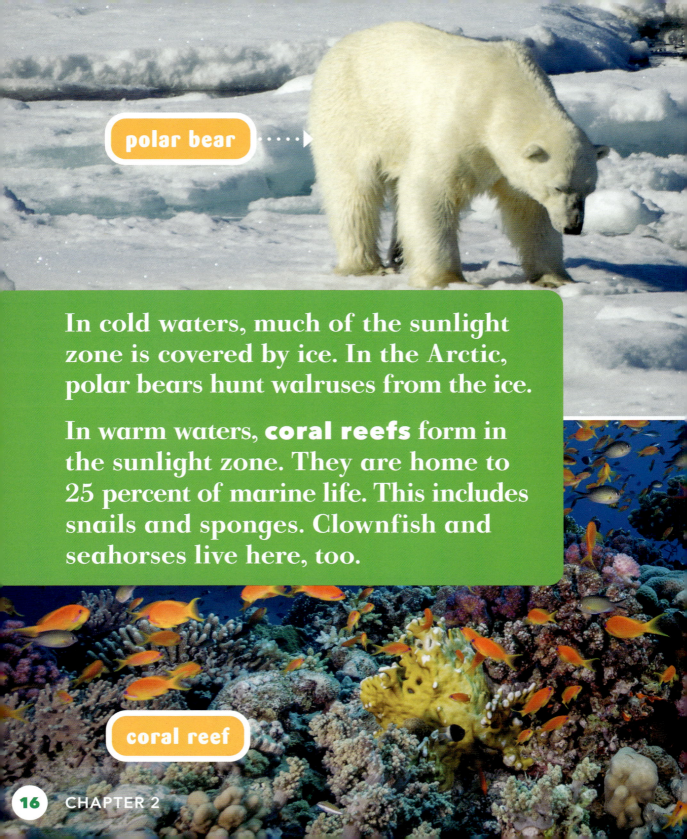

polar bear

In cold waters, much of the sunlight zone is covered by ice. In the Arctic, polar bears hunt walruses from the ice.

In warm waters, **coral reefs** form in the sunlight zone. They are home to 25 percent of marine life. This includes snails and sponges. Clownfish and seahorses live here, too.

coral reef

TAKE A LOOK!

What are some animals that live in each of the ocean's layers? Take a look!

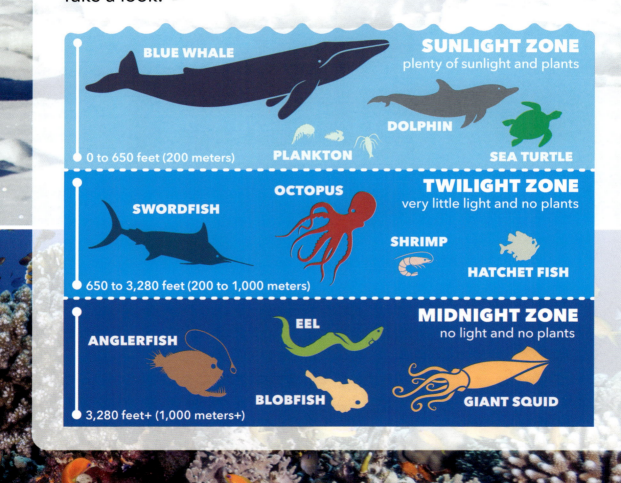

CHAPTER 2   17

CHAPTER 3
THE OCEAN AND US

We have a lot of fun in the ocean. We visit beaches. We swim and sail. We snorkel and surf.

We also get food from the ocean. We catch fish with rods and nets. We eat fish, shellfish, and seaweed.

Scientists have mapped 20 percent of the ocean floor. Maps help us better understand the marine biome. But there is a lot scientists do not know about the ocean. To learn more, they take submarines under the surface.

What more do you want to learn about the marine biome?

DID YOU KNOW?

Climate change is making Earth warmer. The ocean has an important job. It takes heat from the sun. It spreads it around Earth on **currents** to cool us.

ACTIVITIES & TOOLS

TRY THIS!

FORM OCEAN CURRENTS

Currents affect life in and out of the water. Some currents are made when ocean water freezes and pushes warmer water away. Make your own currents in this activity!

What You Need:
- 4 cups of boiling water
- 2 cups of cold water
- 9×13-inch clear baking dish
- blue and red food coloring
- 1 cup of ice
- spoon
- large heat-proof bowl

❶ Ask an adult to help you boil 4 cups of water.

❷ Pour 2 cups of cold water into the baking dish. Add a few drops of blue food coloring.

❸ Add the ice and stir to make the water even colder.

❹ Have an adult pour the boiling water into the large bowl. Add a few drops of red food coloring.

❺ Slowly pour the hot water into a corner of the baking dish filled with cold, blue water. What do you notice? Can you see the currents forming?

GLOSSARY

algae: Small plants without roots or stems that grow mainly in water.

basins: Natural low areas on Earth's surface where water collects.

bay: A portion of the ocean that is partly enclosed by land.

biome: A habitat and everything that lives in it.

climate change: Changes in Earth's weather and climate over time.

continents: The seven large landmasses on Earth.

coral reefs: Long lines of coral that lie in warm, shallow waters.

currents: Movements of water in one direction.

estuaries: Wide parts of rivers, where they meet the ocean.

plankton: Tiny animals and plants that drift or float in oceans and lakes.

predators: Animals that hunt other animals for food.

prey: Animals that are hunted by other animals for food.

shallow: Not deep.

species: One of the groups into which similar animals and plants are divided.

surface: The outermost layer of something.

tides: The constant changes in sea level that are caused by the pull of the sun and moon on Earth.

INDEX

animals 9, 10, 11, 13, 14, 16, 17, 19
Arctic Ocean 6, 7, 16
Atlantic Ocean 6, 7
Bay of Fundy 5
beaches 18
climate change 21
coral reefs 16
currents 21
estuaries 9
ice 16
Indian Ocean 6, 7
midnight zone 14, 17
ocean floor 21
Pacific Ocean 6, 7
plants 13, 14, 17
Red Sea 6, 7
salt water 4
scientists 10, 21
seas 6
Southern Ocean 6, 7
sunlight 13, 14, 17
sunlight zone 13, 16, 17
tides 5
twilight zone 13, 17

TO LEARN MORE

Finding more information is as easy as 1, 2, 3.
1. Go to www.factsurfer.com
2. Enter "marinebiomes" into the search box.
3. Choose your book to see a list of websites.